P9-ARB-032

Our Basic FREEDOMS

# THE RIGHT to PETITION

JENNIFER MASON

Gareth Stevens
PUBLISHING

Please visit our website, www.garethstevens.com.
For a free color catalog of all our high-quality books,
call toll free 1-800-542-2595 or fax 1-877-542-2596.

Cataloging-in-Publication Data

Names: Mason, Jennifer.
Title: The right to petition / Jennifer Mason.
Description: New York : Gareth Stevens Publishing, 2017. | Series: Our basic freedoms | Includes index.
Identifiers: ISBN 9781482461152 (pbk.) | ISBN 9781482461923 (library bound) | ISBN 9781482461145 (6 pack)
Subjects: LCSH: Petition, Right of--United States--History--Juvenile literature. | Petition, Right of--United
States--Juvenile literature.
Classification: LCC KF4778.M2853 2017 | DDC 323.4'8--dc23

Published in 2017 by
**Gareth Stevens Publishing**
111 East 14th Street, Suite 349
New York, NY 10003

Developed and Produced by Focus Strategic Communications, Inc.
Project Manager: Adrianna Edwards
Editor: Ron Edwards
Layout and Composition: Laura Brady, Ruth Dwight
Copyeditors: Adrianna Edwards, Francine Geraci
Media Researchers: Maria DeCambra, Adrianna Edwards
Proofreader: Francine Geraci
Index: Ron Edwards

Photo Credits: Credit Abbreviations: I istock; LOC Library of Congress; NARA National Archives and Records
Administration; S Shutterstock; WC Wikimedia Commons. Position on the page: T: top, C: center, B: bottom,
L: left, R: right. Cover: Peopleimages/I (photo); Jasemin90/S; R: AKaiser/S; 4: Lukas Maverick Greyson/S; 6:
Romakoma/S; 7: Ritu Manoj Jethani/S; 8: Cheryl Casey/S; 9: LOC/LC-USP6-360A; 10 T: Shamleen/S; 10 B:
EdBockStock/S; 11: From the New York Public Library/421668; 12: WC; 13: Jorfer/WC; 14: Georgios Kollidas/S;
15: Everett - Art/S; 16: LOC/LC-USZ62-48883; 17: From the New York Public Library/54390; 18: Daderot/WC;
19 T: Everett Historical/S; 19 B: DFree/S; 20: JPL Designs/S; 21: LOC/LC-DIG-pga-01848; 22: Billion Photos/S;
23: Everett Historical/S; 24: Georgios Kollidas/S; 25: Everett Historical/S; 27: WC; 28: David Evison/S; 29:
Evan El-Amin/S; 30: lpankonin/WC; 32: Everett Historical/S; 33: Everett Historical/S; 34: Everett Historical/S;
35: LOC/LC-USZ62-60139; 36: Nagel Photography/S; 37: National Archives and Records Adminstration/
306-PSD-65-1882 (Box 93); 38: The Library of Virginia/Rice Collection 1852A; 39: LOC/LC-USZ62-84331; 40:
gpointstudio/S; 41: JStone/S; 42: Zack Frank/S; 43 L: Helga Esteb/S; 43 R: Joseph Sohm/S; 44: spwidoff/S; 45:
Defense Video Imagery Distribution System/31860/Photo by SGT Quentin Johnson.

Printed in the United States of America
CPSIA compliance information: Batch CW17GS: For further information contact
Gareth Stevens, New York, New York at 1-800-542-2595.

# CONTENTS

# CHAPTER 1

# THE POWERFUL IMPACT OF PETITIONS

## TRAYVON MARTIN

As the Sunday dusk slid into night on February 26, 2012, 17-year-old Trayvon Martin was shot and killed by George Zimmerman. The tragedy unfolded in Sanford, a central Florida town of 50,000, not far from Orlando and Cape Canaveral. Martin was an unarmed African American high school student who lived in Miami but was visiting his father, who lived nearby. Martin had just bought some Skittles at a convenience store. As he strolled to his dad's house, he chatted on his cell phone with his girlfriend.

Zimmerman, a neighborhood watch volunteer, called local police to report Martin's "suspicious" behavior. Sometime after 7:11 p.m., Zimmerman confronted Martin. The details are unknown, but the two tangled in an altercation and Zimmerman shot and killed Martin. Local police questioned Zimmerman, who admitted to killing Martin. With bleeding wounds on his face and head, Zimmerman claimed self-defense and was released without charge.

Trayvon Martin, shown here as a cardboard photo-realistic figure, was killed by George Zimmerman in February 2012.

## PETITION POWER

The shooting kicked off a series of marches and protests across many US cities. Many people debated the mysterious details, as well as the most critical questions: had Martin died simply because he was black, and did Zimmerman walk free because he wasn't black? More than 1,000 mourners attended Trayvon Martin's funeral. Media coverage was extensive.

## FLOOD OF SIGNATURES

Frustrated by police inaction, Martin's parents, Sybrina Fulton and Tracy Martin, launched an online petition through Change.org. They called for a full investigation. The petition attracted over 2 million signatures of support from around the world. The surge of support led authorities to reopen the case. More than a year after the shooting, authorities charged Zimmerman with murder. Even though Martin was unarmed, a six-person jury deliberated for 2 days before returning a "not guilty" verdict on all counts.

## Fast Fact

### ONLINE PETITIONS

In the past, petition organizers would collect signatures on physical paper by going from door to door or attracting people in crowds. Today, in the Internet age, getting petitions together is much easier and more efficient. Websites such as Change.org, GoPetition, Petitions24, and iPetitions speed up the process, allowing organizers to collect many more signatures online. For example, Change.org claims that more than 150 million people in 196 countries support a variety of causes through their website.

## THIS IS THE RIGHT PLACE

Because petitions are so powerful, many countries punish people who use them. Petitioning the government comes with penalties such as large fines, jail time, or even torture and execution.

The situation is different in the United States thanks to the Bill of Rights. The Bill of Rights generally refers to the first 10 amendments added to the Constitution in 1791. The ideas behind these additions stem from the Framers' belief that "natural rights" were **inherent** in all people and from their preference for constitutionalism, a form of government with limited power.

## Fast Fact

### BILL OF RIGHTS: BEYOND PETITIONS

Some amendments, such as the Fourth Amendment, protect our property—including our bodies, our homes, and our papers. The Sixth Amendment protects our right to a trial if we are accused of a crime and our right to have a lawyer. The Third Amendment prevents the government from putting soldiers in our homes, while the Eighth Amendment prohibits the government from imposing excessive bail or fines, or using cruel or unusual punishment.

# BILL OF RIGHTS PROTECTIONS

The Constitution and the Bill of Rights were written by the Framers, particularly James Madison, to protect what people can do and outline what the government cannot do. They were originally written to apply only to the federal government. However, after the Fourteenth Amendment, which granted citizenship to former slaves, was passed in 1868, the clauses in the Bill of Rights applied to state and local governments, too.

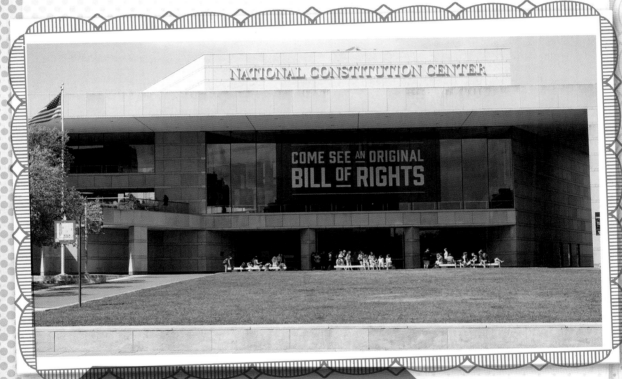

The National Constitution Center in Philadelphia has on display one of the 12 surviving copies of the Bill of Rights. The Center first opened its doors on July 4, 2003.

## FIRST OF ALL

"Congress shall make no law respecting an establishment of religion, or prohibiting the free exercise thereof; or **abridging** the freedom of speech, or of the press; or the right of the people peaceably to assemble, and to petition the Government for a redress of grievances."

That is the exact wording of the First Amendment. As you can see, it grants a lot of freedoms, including petitioning. Or, more accurately, it restricts the government from hindering a person's religious practices or what a person has to say or wants to write. Additionally, the government cannot prevent anyone from assembling for meetings or protests.

The 10 amendments in the Bill of Rights traveled a long road. They were debated from 1787 through 1788. They were put up for approval in 1789. Finally, they were **ratified** in their present form in 1791.

## COPIES OF THE BILL OF RIGHTS

In 1791, Congress dispatched 14 copies of the proposed Bill of Rights—one copy for each of the original 13 states, and one for the federal government, as part of the ratification process. On December 15, 1791, all parties agreed to the 10 amendments that we call the Bill of Rights, and they were added to the Constitution. Over the years, the original ratification copies sent to Georgia, Maryland, New York, and Pennsylvania inexplicably disappeared. A fifth copy had gone missing from North Carolina.

## Fast Fact

### LOST DOCUMENT

In 1865, a sheepskin copy of the Bill of Rights was stolen from the statehouse in Raleigh, North Carolina. It was thought to be lost forever. Amazingly, in 2003—138 years later—the document resurfaced! Wayne Pratt, a New England antique dealer and a regular on the *Antiques Road Show*, tried to sell it to the National Constitution Center museum in Philadelphia. The FBI and other authorities got involved. After much legal wrangling, in 2007, Pratt agreed to donate the copy back to North Carolina.

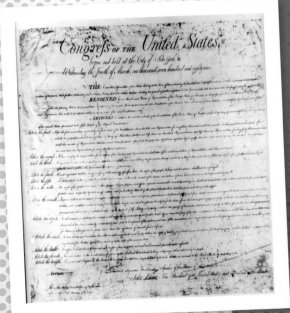

## GETTING INVOLVED

Petitioning is more than just adding your name to an online list or a sheet of paper. It is your right to complain without facing punishment. It also includes lobbying, writing letters, e-mail campaigns, testifying, peaceful protests, **picketing**, or filing a lawsuit to sue a person, a company, or even the government.

There are many ways to get people interested in causes, petitions, and taking action.

## RIGHTS GO HAND IN HAND

In a way, the right to petition combines our right to free speech with our right to assemble. That is, we can bring many voices together to speak freely.

To really understand how this right makes us unique as a country, we need to trace where the notion of petitioning comes from. To appreciate what we have, we first need to see what was missing.

The Declaration of Independence, portrayed here being signed by the Framers in 1776, remains one of the world's most revolutionary petitions, calling for an all-new way of governing, thinking, and living freely.

# CHAPTER 2

# PETITIONS AND LIMITED GOVERNMENT

### KING JOHN RELENTS

In 1215, in a soggy meadow aptly named Runnymede, 25 rebel barons confronted England's unpopular King John. They gave the king a list of complaints with demands to make changes—or else!

King John was extremely unpopular. He had waged a lot of battles, which was, back then, a super "kingly" thing to do. Unfortunately, many of King John's military campaigns flopped. Just the year before, he had suffered a huge defeat in the Battle of Bouvines and had to give up English territory in Northern France. To top it all off, his wars were expensive, and he taxed his subjects mercilessly. The rebellious barons were dissatisfied with all this and more. Perhaps wisely, King John put down his sword and picked up a quill.

The rebel barons forced the unpopular King John to sign the Magna Carta, "the Great Charter," in June 1215.

## THE RULE OF LAW

By signing the barons' document, the Magna Carta, King John essentially acknowledged that the rule of law presided over everyone—commoner, knight, or king. To abide by this rule of law, the king had to surrender portions of his once limitless powers. He could no longer arrest someone simply because he did not like them or their pointy shoes. And, perhaps most important to the barons, the king could not punish a subject for petitioning him with complaints.

A Magna Carta replica and display is seen here in the rotunda of the United States Capitol in Washington, DC. This copy of the Magna Carta is one of four made of the original document that was signed more than 800 years ago.

## Fast Fact

### DIVINE RIGHT OF KINGS

Beginning in the Middle Ages, **monarchs** were thought to have derived their power and authority directly from God, not from the people or from other earthly groups. As a result, these rulers were considered sacred and accountable only to God, not to the people.

# A SIGNATURE IDEA

That a monarch would agree to have his divine powers limited by the people he ruled was unthinkable. That people could complain about and to their government without penalty was unheard of.

Nonetheless, once signed by King John, the radical notions stated in the Magna Carta settled deep into Western culture. In fact, petitioning as a right crossed over the Atlantic when England established **colonies** in the Americas. In 1641, the Massachusetts Body of Liberties became the first royal **charter** establishing a colony in which the people's right to petition was fully protected. In court, at town meetings, in writing, or aloud, the people were free to present information, pose questions, deliver a motion, file a complaint, offer a bill of law, or hand in an actual petition.

## SIGNIFICANCE OF THE MAGNA CARTA

Some historians see the Magna Carta as a great turning point in the history of Britain, the West, and democracy in general because a king was forced to acknowledge the **secular**, or non-religious, power of the people. Many saw the signing as a significant milestone in the political development of constitutional government in England. That is, it marks the rise of limited governance.

Sir Walter Scott's 1820 novel *Ivanhoe* established King John's (pictured here) reputation as a cowardly, sadistic villain. This depiction carried over into many of the popular Robin Hood plays and Hollywood movies.

## BLACKSTONE'S *COMMENTARIES*

Sir William Blackstone (1723–1780) was a pioneering legal scholar. His legal guide, *Commentaries on the Laws of England* (1765), remained in print until the middle of the twentieth century. His writings had enormous influence in the United States—influencing political greats from Alexander Hamilton and John Adams to Abraham Lincoln. In his *Commentaries*, Blackstone reveals how commonplace the once-radical idea of petitioning had become in the 5½ centuries since the barons met King John at Runnymede.

## A BROKEN OLIVE BRANCH

Across the Atlantic, disgruntled colonists petitioned King George III repeatedly to overturn what they called the Intolerable Acts—laws, requirements, and restrictions the British government imposed on their lifestyles and livelihoods, including restricted trade, sharing their homes with soldiers, unfair taxation, and limits on buying land. Unlike King John, George III ignored the petitions and paid a hefty price for it.

King George III of the United Kingdom (1738–1820) is often blamed for the American Revolutionary War.

# DICKINSON'S PETITIONS

The conflict between Britain and the American colonies escalated throughout the 1770s. Many colonists increasingly called for independence, while British authorities called for an increasingly forceful crackdown. Some colonists, including John Adams, believed a war was inevitable. Others, however, such as John Dickinson, hoped to compromise and work out any differences.

Dickinson was largely responsible for two major petitions meant to calm the crisis. The first was the Petition to the King (1774). It called for the repeal of the Coercive Acts and stressed the colonists' desire to remain loyal subjects of the British monarchy. Neither the king nor the British Parliament gave a formal reply to the petition.

The second document became known as the Olive Branch Petition. Dickinson drafted it with help from Thomas Jefferson. The Olive Branch was a last-ditch effort to avoid a full-scale revolt and war with Britain.

John Dickinson (1732–1808) was the author of two petitions to King George III.

# REVOLT

Despite the best effort of moderates like Dickinson, British troops skirmished with colonial militias at Lexington and Concord, Massachusetts, in April 1775. After that, there was no turning back. The colonies revolted. They declared their independence on July 4, 1776. Over the next 5 years, muskets fired and cannons boomed until British forces surrendered on October 19, 1781, at Yorktown, Virginia. With the fighting at an end, both sides endured 2 more years of diplomatic negotiations before signing the Treaty of Paris, which formally ended the American Revolutionary War.

Once the ash and shrapnel settled, the former colonies established an all-new form of government, never before seen anywhere in the world.

The Battles of Lexington and Concord in 1775 were the first of the American Revolution. The opening rifle shot from the colonists at the Battle of Concord is often described as "the shot heard round the world."

# CHAPTER 3

# NATURAL RIGHTS IN THE NEW NATION

## DISCORD AND DISUNITY

After the Revolutionary War, the colonies became independent states, each with the power to make its own laws. Under the Articles of Confederation (1781), the states agreed to come together in a loose union, presided over by a weak federal government. The Founders, reeling from the abuses of power suffered under British rule, deliberately designed that central government to be weak. Unfortunately, what sounded good on paper did not work in real life. The Continental Congress struggled to make everyone get along.

About 6 years later, the "united" states were in crisis. The league of friends squabbled like enemies. Congress had no power to collect taxes, pay bills, regulate trade, or even defend itself from potential invasion. In short, the new nation was strapped in every way. In May 1787, state delegates held a Constitutional Convention in the hope of solving these problems.

After 4 months of work—in the sweltering heat of a Philadelphia summer—the delegates emerged with four sheets of parchment on which were written the words of the US Constitution.

# ALEXANDER HAMILTON

Alexander Hamilton was a driving force behind the formation of a Constitutional Convention. He advocated for a strong central government.

Alexander Hamilton appears on the face of the $10 bill.

## Fast Fact

### HAMILTON: AN AMERICAN MUSICAL

Alexander Hamilton's pivotal role in shaping the new nation is portrayed in the Broadway musical *Hamilton: An American Musical*. Lin-Manuel Miranda (pictured here) wrote and starred in this smash hit. The US Treasury had planned to replace Hamilton on the $10 bill, but because of the popularity of the musical, Alexander Hamilton's image will remain.

## BRIEF, FOCUSED STRATEGY

In 4,543 words—including the signatures—the Constitution established a central, or federal, government structured with plenty of ways to limit its powers. This unique, revolutionary, world-changing document nestled cozily across four pages of parchment. Parchment, or treated animal skin such as sheepskin, was widely used to record important documents because it was so durable.

The Constitution also created an indivisible union of the states under or alongside a federal government. The federal government saw the states unified under its power, while the states saw themselves equal in power, standing shoulder-to-shoulder with the federal government.

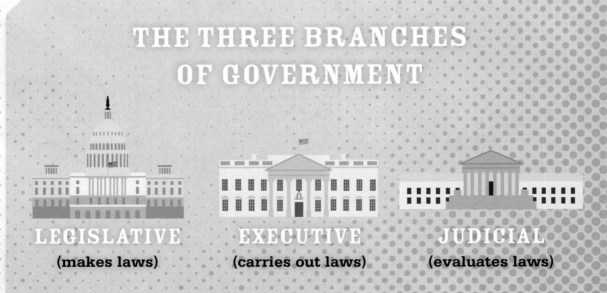

## THE THREE BRANCHES OF GOVERNMENT

**LEGISLATIVE**
(makes laws)

**EXECUTIVE**
(carries out laws)

**JUDICIAL**
(evaluates laws)

# FEDERAL VERSUS STATE POWER

Debates about which level of government controls which powers continue to the present day. At the time of the Revolution, there was a great deal of debate over the benefits and consequences of a weak or a strong central government. Federalists, such as Hamilton and Adams, favored more power for the central government. Not surprisingly, the Anti-Federalists, including Thomas Jefferson and Patrick Henry, favored the opposite. They preferred states to be stronger. James Madison, author of the Bill of Rights, was against the idea of too much power settling in any one place. This belief influenced his wording of the amendments.

These opposing views continued to simmer under the surface for the next 75 years. When the conflict finally erupted in the Civil War (1861–1865), it left a sizable wound on America's landscape. Battlefields were piled with hundreds of thousands of dead soldiers, so bloody that you could not determine whether their uniforms were blue or gray.

Here, General Phillip Sheridan charges forward at the US Civil War Battle of Five Forks in April 1865.

## THE WAR OF THE WORDS

In a sense, the young nation tore itself apart because it could not agree on whether the power of the states sat *under* the power of the federal government or *alongside* it. Why would a country go to such extremes over a couple of prepositions? It's a fair question. Part of the problem rests in the Constitution's length. The Constitution may be brief, but that does not mean it is easy to read or understand. Some of its terms were legal jargon, such as "ex post facto" or "letters of mark and reprisal." Other words were just murky. For example, what is a "bill of attainder" or "privileges and immunities"?

## Fast Fact

### INK AND QUILLS

The Constitution was written on parchment using ink and a feather quill. Turkey, peacock, ostrich, and pheasant feathers made excellent quills as long as the writer shaved away the barbs—sharp points that could rub the writer's hands raw. At the time the Constitution was written, the most popular ink was made from iron salts, tannins, and resin or sap. From the twelfth to the nineteenth centuries, the quill and ink combo was the most popular way to write. But it could also be messy! Too much ink splattered the parchment, while a dull quill point slopped out soggy letters.

## WHO ARE "PEOPLE"?

The word "people" in the Constitution is tough to unpack. Women and people of color were not considered "people." They were thought of as lesser beings—less able and less smart. Young people were also not fully "people." They had to be a certain age before they could enjoy all the liberties guaranteed in the Bill of Rights. Extending the bounty of freedom to a select few while denying it to others flew in the face of natural rights.

Northern **abolitionists**—people and groups, such as the American Anti-Slavery Society—flooded Congress with thousands of petitions calling for an end to slavery. Yet Congress ignored these petitions because its pro-slavery groups instituted a "gag rule." That means they barred every single one of the petitions from being read, let alone discussed or debated.

Fast Fact

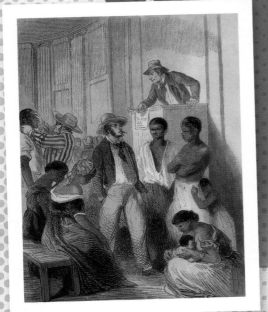

### THE ABOLITIONIST MOVEMENT

The movement to abolish the international slave trade had its roots in seventeenth-century England. Britain led the way when it outlawed trading slaves in 1807 and, 25 years later, abolished slavery completely throughout its empire. America had to fight a long and bloody civil war before it rid itself of the despised institution.

## COMING TO TERMS

The concept of natural rights took shape in the 1600s. Several English and Scottish writers and philosophers—including James Harrington, Algernon Sidney, David Hume, and John Locke—speculated that all people were born with rights, in the same way they were born with toenails or lungs.

Although Algernon Sidney died long before any of the Founding Fathers of the American Revolution were born, the English political theorist and philosopher contributed greatly to the emerging ideologies on governments formed of the people, by the people, and for the people, also known as **republicanism**. His *Discourses Concerning Government*, published in 1698, has been called the "textbook of the American Revolution."

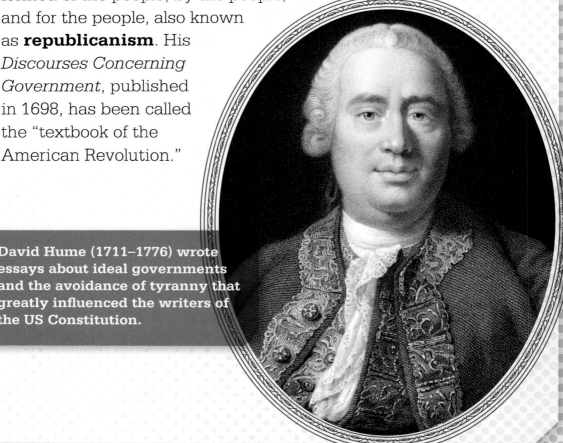

David Hume (1711–1776) wrote essays about ideal governments and the avoidance of tyranny that greatly influenced the writers of the US Constitution.

# JOHN LOCKE

A few years earlier, John Locke had published *Two Treatises of Government* (1689). In the second treatise, he asserted that regardless of someone's class or nationality, all people were endowed with rights to life, liberty, and property. They had these rights simply because they were alive and human. In a sense, natural rights are like air— fundamental, essential, and naturally part of life.

In his *Treatises*, Locke declared, "It is evident that all human beings—as creatures belonging to the same species and rank and born indiscriminately with all the same natural advantages and faculties—are equal amongst themselves."

The Constitution included these natural rights and promised them to all people. Unfortunately, the promise existed only on paper. In practice, only a few "people" enjoyed their natural rights, while other "people" went without. In 1854, a radical petition landed before the Supreme Court, forcing the nation to come to terms with the precise meanings of its core beliefs.

John Locke was an English philosopher. His ideas on natural rights deeply influenced many of the Framers of the American Constitution.

# CHAPTER 4
# THE SUPREME COURT

## COURTING DISASTER

In general, courts are where people go when they have a disagreement about what laws mean and whether laws were broken. Some courts are designed to handle very specific legal matters such as taxes, bankruptcy, or family matters such as divorce. State, district, and municipal courts are limited by their jurisdiction, or the reach of their legal power. For instance, state courts deal only with state laws.

US Supreme Court

US Appeals Courts

US District Courts

**THE US FEDERAL COURT SYSTEM**

State Supreme Courts

State Appeals Courts

State District Courts

**THE STATE COURT SYSTEM**

## HOW COURTS WORK

Some courts hear trials. Others hear **appeals**. Trial courts are a lot like what you might see in movies, where the two arguing sides—the prosecution/plaintiff and the defense—present evidence for their side of the argument, or "case," to a judge and jury, who then deliver a decision, or "ruling." If either the prosecution/plaintiff or the defense does not agree with that decision, they can appeal it. That means they can ask an appellate court to review the decision to see if a mistake was made.

## Fast Fact

### COURT COSTUMES

Think "judge" and you're likely to picture a person in a black robe. Judges and their robes date back to the 1300s in England, when the proper attire for anyone attending the royal court generally

included a long robe, a hood, and a cloak. In the United States, Supreme Court justices used to mimic British judges, sporting red robes trimmed with soft white fur, their heads topped with white powdered wigs, also known as perukes. Chief Justice John Marshall, who led the Court from 1801 to 1835, made the switch to the wigless, plain black robe look we see today.

## HEARING APPEALS

The Supreme Court is an appellate court, which means it hears only appeals from other courts. Every year, between 7,000 and 8,000 cases are submitted to the Supreme Court. However, it chooses about 80 of those. Usually, the Court selects cases that will have the broadest national impact. Whenever disputes erupt over the exact meaning of the words in the Constitution, the Supreme Court steps in to deliver an exact interpretation. Not only that, once the Supreme Court makes a decision, no other court can overturn it.

## Fast Fact

### THE US SUPREME COURT BUILDING

The US Supreme Court Building, located in Washington, DC, looks like an ancient Roman temple with its white marble columns and sweeping front steps. Far from ancient, the building was completed in 1935. Before that, the Court had bounced around New York and Pennsylvania and various places in Washington, DC. No one thought to give the Supreme Court its own building until former President William Howard Taft became the Chief Justice in 1921. Unfortunately, Taft died before the US Supreme Court Building was completed.

# JUSTICES OF THE SUPREME COURT

There are nine justices on the Supreme Court, and the one appointed to be the leader is called the Chief Justice. Once the Supreme Court has decided to hear a case, the justices receive written arguments, known as briefs, from each side of the case. Finally, the lawyers for both sides present oral arguments.

## ANTONIN SCALIA

Antonin Scalia died in February 2016 at the age of 79. He is seen in a 2007 oil painting, displayed at his funeral in the Great Hall of the Supreme Court. Scalia was appointed to the Supreme Court in 1986 by Ronald Reagan and served for nearly 30 years (10,732 days) as Supreme Court justice. But he ranks only number 15 by length of term of justices. In first place is William O. Douglas, who served 13,358 days between 1939 and 1975. Scalia was known as a defender of executive power (even when he disagreed with the president's opinion). However, at the same time, he defended states' rights against federal powers.

## DECISIONS AND OPINIONS

After oral arguments, the justices take their time to issue a decision. They can spend a week or several months reviewing all the information in a case. When the justices are ready, they each cast a vote. The side with the most votes wins the appeal.

Once the votes are cast, the Supreme Court must write up its opinion. Usually, the Chief Justice selects a justice to write the opinion. When the ruling is extremely controversial or complicated, the Chief Justice often writes the opinion.

## Fast Fact

### US SUPREME COURT SEAL

The Seal of the Supreme Court was created between 1776 and 1782. It features a bald eagle, the national bird of the United States. The 13 stars above the eagle's head, as well as the 13 red and white stripes on the shield and the 13 arrows in the eagle's left talon, all represent the 13 original states. Interestingly, the motto, *E pluribus unum*, which is Latin for "out of many, one," uses 13 letters.

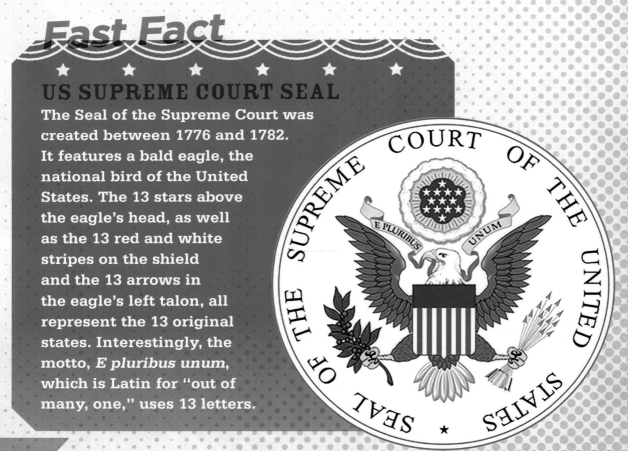

## OPINIONS AND DISSENTS

Writing the opinion involves clearly explaining how and why the Court came to its decision—how it interpreted the language of the Constitution, the logic it used, and the precedents it followed. Following precedent means that the justices look back on previous Supreme Court decisions and use those as a guide. Finally, the justices who disagree with the judgment can write a dissenting (differing) opinion.

**SUPREME COURT PROCESS**

Briefs

Oral Arguments

Votes

Opinions

?

Dissents
(optional)

## A DRED-FULL DECISION

In 1854, a slave named Dred Scott sued the man who owned him. Scott originally lived in Missouri, a state where slavery was legal. But he was taken to Illinois and the Wisconsin Territory, both places where slavery had been banned. Scott insisted he was now a free man.

The Court ruled against Scott. In a notorious opinion for the Court, Chief Justice Roger Taney claimed that slaves were not citizens. They had zero right to petition the federal or state governments with lawsuits.

As a result, the dispute over slavery escalated between the federal government and the slave-owning states. Seeing the states as unified under it, the government felt it had the power to ban slavery. Believing themselves equal alongside the government, the slave states saw the ban as unconstitutional.

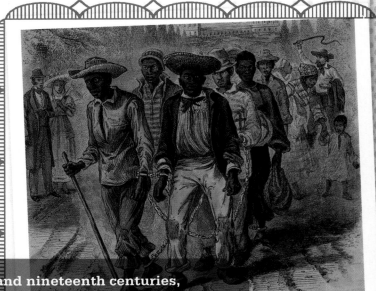

Between the sixteenth and nineteenth centuries, about 12.5 million people were kidnapped and shipped to the Americas as slaves. There, they were forced to undertake brutal physical labor and harsh treatment. Slaves are shown here traveling in a chained line, while a man cracks a whip at their backs.

## CIVIL WAR

Finally, in 1861, the debate sparked the Civil War. The "united" states were divided. After more than 4 years of battle, the slave states lost in 1865. Congress added the Thirteenth, Fourteenth, and Fifteenth Amendments to the Bill of Rights in order to ban slavery completely, extend citizenship to former slaves, and guarantee their voting rights. But again, the victory was confined to words on paper. In everyday life, enjoying natural rights continued to elude entire groups of people.

## Fast Fact

### CIVIL WAR CASUALTIES

The Civil War was brutal. In just 4 years, the Union and Confederate armies suffered many casualties, including more than 620,000 deaths. Compare that to all other American wars (from the Revolution to the War in Afghanistan), in which about 650,000 lives were lost. The Battle of Gettysburg stands out among the deadliest, with 50,000 casualties piling up in 3 days. On November 19, 1863, Abraham Lincoln delivered a 2-minute speech that would become one of the most famous orations in history. The Gettysburg Address, as it is known, was so named to commemorate the tragic loss of life not just in the 3-day battle at Gettysburg, Pennsylvania, but also in the ongoing worldwide battle for human equality.

# CHAPTER 5

# COURT GAME CHANGERS

## JIM CROW LAWS

In the century after the Civil War, many southern states found ways to get around the protections guaranteed in the Bill of Rights plus the trio of new amendments. Many passed **segregation** laws, also known as Jim Crow laws. "Jim Crow" was a hateful term referring to black people. Under Jim Crow laws, people of color were given supposedly equal but separate everything: schools, pools, stores, and seats on trains and buses.

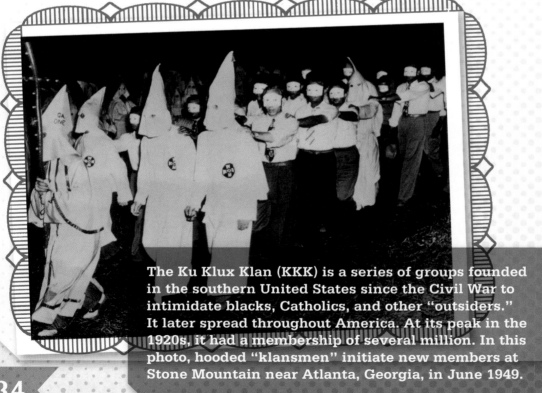

The Ku Klux Klan (KKK) is a series of groups founded in the southern United States since the Civil War to intimidate blacks, Catholics, and other "outsiders." It later spread throughout America. At its peak in the 1920s, it had a membership of several million. In this photo, hooded "klansmen" initiate new members at Stone Mountain near Atlanta, Georgia, in June 1949.

## SEGREGATION

Separate rarely proved equal. This was especially true in segregated schools. The conditions in classrooms were deplorable, at best. Students lacked the books, supplies, and sometimes teachers essential for learning. In 1954, in *Brown v. Board of Education of Topeka*, the Supreme Court ruled that any and all segregation was unconstitutional.

## Fast Fact

### THURGOOD MARSHALL

Supreme Court Justice Thurgood Marshall was the great-grandson of a slave. He became the first African American justice on the Supreme Court, serving from 1967 to 1991. Before that, he was a lawyer, providing free legal help to poor black people. He won 29 of the 32 cases he argued before the Supreme Court. His biggest victory of all: *Brown v. Board of Education*.

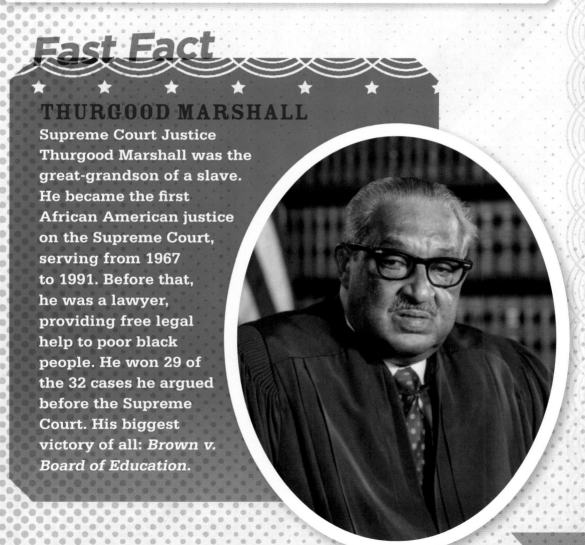

# THE LITTLE ROCK NINE

On September 4, 1957, six young women and three young men set off for their first day of school at Central High School in Little Rock, Arkansas. Minnijean, Elizabeth, Thelma, Melba, Gloria, and Carlotta hugged their books tight against the buttons on their blouses. Terrance, Ernest, and Jefferson lugged their books at their sides, trying to appear at ease. All wore their finest—slacks and button-up shirts for the boys, pleated and flared skirts for the girls—but nothing could cover up their nervousness.

This memorial to the Little Rock Nine was unveiled on the grounds of the Arkansas State Capitol building in Little Rock, Arkansas, on January 15, 2014.

## SCHOOL OBSTRUCTION

The six-story Central High rose before them like a castle with its reflecting pond, sweeping terraced stairways, mighty windows, carved stone arches, and columns. But the students could not gain entry to the stately campus. A snarling mob and a rigid line of National Guard troops blocked the way.

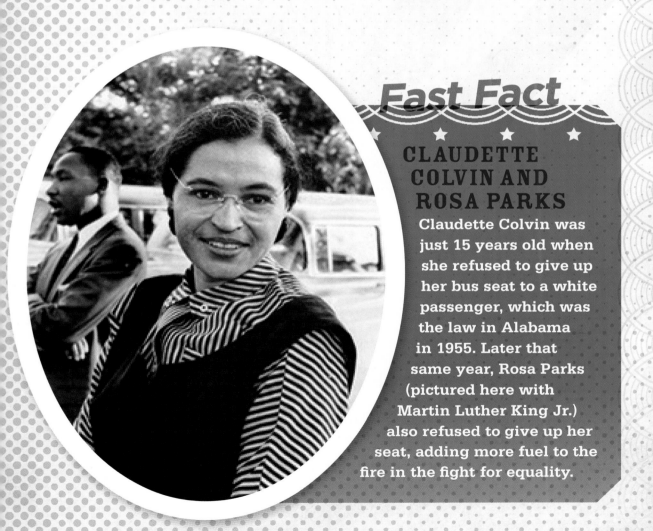

## Fast Fact

### ★ ★ ★
### CLAUDETTE COLVIN AND ROSA PARKS

Claudette Colvin was just 15 years old when she refused to give up her bus seat to a white passenger, which was the law in Alabama in 1955. Later that same year, Rosa Parks (pictured here with Martin Luther King Jr.) also refused to give up her seat, adding more fuel to the fire in the fight for equality.

## WHITE BARRIER

The students were barred from setting even a toe on the school grounds that day. Not because they had poor grades. Not because they wore the wrong clothes. Simply because they were black. The mob did not care about the *Brown v. Board of Education* ruling, which was just 3 years old. Their hateful and fearful **prejudice** drove them to defy the law and terrorize nine children.

Jim Crow laws authorized the segregation by race of all institutions such as this school, Navy Hill School in Richmond, Virginia, in 1958.

## MILITARY AID

Luckily, President Dwight D. Eisenhower responded to the crisis. Urged on by the famous civil rights leader, Dr. Martin Luther King Jr., Eisenhower took control of Arkansas' National Guard. On September 23, he sent the troops back to the school—only this time they were ordered to hold back the mob and protect the nine students.

Flanked on both sides by soldiers, the nine students entered Central High School, officially beginning the hopeful process of integration.

The nine African American students enrolled in Little Rock Central High, an all-white school, but were prevented from attending. In September 1957, President Eisenhower (shown here) ordered soldiers to escort the students to class.

## THE CIVIL RIGHTS ACT

Finally, in 1965, Congress passed the Civil Rights Act (CRA). The CRA completely outlawed discrimination on the basis of race, color, religion, sex, or national **creed**. Inclusion, not seclusion, drove America out of the past and into the future. Differences were to be embraced rather than punished or corrected through hateful or violent actions. Most importantly, all people were to be counted as human beings with full access to their natural rights.

But, equality in the United States could not mature without first enduring many ugly events and moments.

Youth everywhere rebelled against the confines of society in the 1960s. Growing long hair and wearing unusual clothing were signs of rebellion.

# WOMEN'S RIGHTS

These days, American women enjoy seemingly boundless freedoms. They run multimillion-dollar businesses, serve on the Supreme Court, and legislate in government. They make life-saving discoveries in science and medicine. Some blast off into outer space. Others win Olympic Gold Medals.

In order to enjoy these many freedoms, countless predecessors fought hard and frequently exercised their right to petition in order to change the old status quo. For decades, activists picketed, protested, wrote letters, went on hunger strikes, and even burned their clothing, all to gain equal rights and equal treatment under the law. After all, the Fifteenth Amendment applied only to black *men*, not women.

Olympic gymnasts Kyla Ross, Aly Raisman, Jordyn Wieber, Gabby Douglas, and McKayla Maroney are shown here in New York City in 2012.

## WOMEN ACTIVISTS

In the 1800s, women, of any color, could not vote. Nor could they earn wages, own property, study at universities, or play sports. By 1920, thanks to the tireless efforts of **suffragists** such as Elizabeth Cady Stanton, Lucretia Mott, and Susan B. Anthony, the Nineteenth Amendment was passed, guaranteeing all women the right to vote. However, the victory was short-lived. Negative gender stereotypes stalled all efforts to pass another amendment that would have ensured equality regardless of sex. All seemed lost on the women's rights front.

This sculpture, "The First Wave" by Lloyd Lillie, includes life-sized bronze statues of Elizabeth Cady Stanton (far left) and Lucretia Mott, women's rights pioneers. The sculpture is on display in the Women's Rights National Historical Park in Seneca Falls, New York.

## STRANGE TWIST

In 1972, a strange twist of events leveled the playing field. Literally. While voting to continue spending for schools, Congress approved a little provision called Title IX. Essentially, Title IX promised that equal money be spent on, and offered to, female students and athletes. That little promise spurred a sporting revolution. Women and girls across the country flocked to sports like never before.

Title IX not only opened the door for some of the world's most celebrated athletes—Serena Williams, Simone Biles, Claressa Shields, Carli Lloyd—but also allowed the world to see women as powerful, capable, and equal to men. Or at the very least, more equal than before.

Hillary Clinton is a former US Secretary of State, US senator, and First Lady. In 2016, she ran as the Democratic candidate in the presidential election. She is shown here at the first CNN Democratic Debate in Las Vegas, Nevada, in October 2015.

Oprah Winfrey, a media personality and philanthropist, is one of the most successful people in America. She is shown here at a reception for her Oprah Winfrey Network (OWN) in Pasadena, California, in January 2011.

# CHAPTER 6

# CONCLUSION

### EQUALITY ENLISTED

As you can see, throughout the centuries, petitions have proven to be powerful tools. In our local communities, we can use petitions to spotlight important issues such as recycling, permitting the prom king to wear a dress (if he wants to), or even race relations that lead to unwarranted violence, as in the case of Trayvon Martin. Most recently, student "clicktivists"—activists who drive change through online petitions—compelled their schools to change unfair rules or remove controversial statues, slogans, or mascots.

Students can use petitions to encourage their local community groups to enforce recycling efforts.

## PETITIONS ON A GREATER SCALE

On an even greater scale, petitions compel kings to surrender. They spur rebellions and revolutions. They stop terrible injustices such as slavery, segregation, and discrimination.

In fact, the right to petition seems to be the key that unlocks all the other rights protected by the First Amendment. Why speak, why publish, why assemble against the government if all such actions will only be silenced or punished? By turning the one small voice into a thunderous majority, the right to petition ensures that a government will always hear what "we, the people" have to say.

Demonstrations, political protests, and vocal assemblies, all forms of petitioning, have become commonplace across the nation. In the virtual and actual worlds, young people now lead the way in uniting to make their voices heard.

# GLOSSARY

**abolitionist**—a person who supports ending slavery

**abridge**—to make shorter, as in "abridged books"

**appeal**—a request for help

**charter**—an official document that explains rights or duties

**colonies**—places where a group of people are sent to settle

**creed**—a set of beliefs held by a person or a group

**inherent**—an essential or inborn element or feature

**monarchs**—rulers who control a kingdom or empire, such as kings, queens, and emperors

**picket**—to stand or walk side-by-side in protest, resembling a picket fence

**prejudice**—an opinion or assumption based on limited knowledge or understanding

**ratify**—to give legal or official approval

**republicanism**—an ideology that supports a government made of elected officials chosen from among the public, or the people

**secular**—nonreligious issues or concerns

**segregation**—the practice of separating people into groups, usually based on race or class

**suffragist**—a person who supports suffrage, or the right to vote, for women

# FURTHER INFORMATION

## Books

Hennessey, Jonathan, and Aaron McConnell. *The Gettysburg Address: A Graphic Adaptation*. New York: HarperCollins, 2013.

Macy, Sue. *Wheels of Change: How Women Rode the Bicycle to Freedom (With a Few Flat Tires Along the Way)*. Washington, DC: National Geographic Society, 2011.

Sheinkin, Steve. *The Port Chicago 50: Disaster, Mutiny, and the Fight for Civil Rights*. New York: Roaring Brook Press, 2014.

## Online

Bill of Rights Institute
www.billofrightsinstitute.org

Center for Civic Education
www.civiced.org

C-SPAN Classroom
www.c-spanclassroom.org

Library of Congress
www.loc.gov/families

National Archives
www.archives.gov

Oyez Project at IIT Chicago-Kent College of Law
www.oyez.org

# INDEX